DATE DUE

597.8   *BC#34880000023874 $28.21*
SPI   Spilsbury, Richard
             Classifying amphibians

Morrill E.S.
Chicago Public Schools
1431 North Leamington Avenue
Chicago, IL 60651

Classifying Amphibians

RICHARD AND LOUISE SPILSBURY

Heinemann Library
Chicago, Illinois

© 2003
Heinemann Library
a division of Reed Elsevier Inc.
Chicago, Illinois

Customer Service 888-454-2279

Visit our website at www.heinemannlibrary.com

Originated by Dot Gradations
Printed in China

07 06 05
10 9 8 7 6 5 4 3

Library of Congress Cataloging-in-Publication Data
Spilsbury, Louise.
    Classifying Amphibians / Louise and Richard Spilsbury.
        p. cm. -- (Classifying living things)
Summary: Explains what amphibians are and how they differ from other animals, offering an overview of the life cycle of several types of amphibians.
Includes bibliographical references and index (p.   ).
    ISBN 1-4034-0845-9 (lib. bdg : hardcover) -- ISBN 1-4034-3343-7 (pbk.)
    1. Amphibians--Classification--Juvenile literature. 2.
Amphibians--Juvenile literature. [1. Amphibians.] I. Spilsbury,
Richard. II. Title. III. Series.
    QL 645 .S64 2003
    597.8--dc21

                                                    2002015397

Acknowledgments
The publishers would like to thank the following for permission to reproduce photographs:
p. 4 Oxford Scientific Films/Zig Leszczynski; p. 5 Nature Picture Library/Geoff Dore; p. 6 Oxford Scientific Films/Mark Hamblin; pp. 7, 22 Oxford Scientific Films; pp. 8, 9 Bruce Coleman/Jane Burton; p. 10 Nature Picture Library/Adrian Davies; p. 11 Bruce Coleman/Robert Maier; p. 12 Oxford Scientific Films/M. Wendler/Okapia; p. 13 Corbis/FPLA; p. 14 Digital Stock; pp. 15, 17 Corbis/Michael and Patricia Fogden; p. 16 Oxford Scientific Films/Juan M. Renjifo; p. 18 Bruce Coleman/MPL Fogden; p. 19 NHPA/Daniel Heuclin; p. 20 Nature Picture Library/Jim Hallet; p. 21 Corbis/Kevin Schafer; p. 23 NHPA/T. Kitchin and V. Hurst; p. 24 Oxford Scientific Films/Professor Jack Dermid; p. 25 Nature Picture Library/Pete Oxford; p. 26 Nature Picture Library/Morley Read; p. 27 Corbis; p. 28 Nature Picture Library; p. 29 RSPCA.

Cover photograph of a society of common frogs in a pond reproduced with permission of the Bruce Coleman Collection/Felix Labhardt.

For Miles and Harriet, toad enthusiasts.

The publishers would like to thank Catherine Armstrong for her assistance in the preparation of this book.

Some words are shown in bold, **like this.** You can find out what they mean by looking in the glossary.

Contents

How Classification Works

The earth is populated with an immense variety of living things, from the largest whale to the tiniest insect. Scientists believe that all these **organisms** are the **descendants** of one group of very simple organisms that lived millions of years ago.

Classification can help us to understand how different organisms might be related to each other. It can also help us make sense of the great variety of organisms, by sorting them into groups.

Sorting life

Different living things are grouped according to the characteristics, or features, that they have in common. Some of these are obvious at first glance. For example, any animal you see that has feathers is a bird.

However, there are many characteristics that scientists use to classify living things that are not so obvious. Fish, mammals, reptiles, birds, and amphibians are grouped together because they are all **vertebrates.** Other less obvious characteristics can be used to divide organisms into smaller groups. These include how they **reproduce,** how they breathe, and the type of skin they have.

There are many different ways to classify, and scientists often disagree about the best way. Nevertheless, over time scientists have come up with a way of sorting all organisms.

The salamander looks a bit like a lizard, but it is an amphibian. It has characteristics in common with all other amphibians.

From kingdoms to species

Living things are generally divided into huge groups called kingdoms. Plants, for example, are all grouped in one kingdom, and all animals in another. Each kingdom is divided into smaller groups, each called a **phylum**. A phylum is divided into **classes**, classes into **orders**, orders into **families**, families into **genera**, and genera into **species**. A species is a single kind of organism, such as a natterjack toad.

Common and scientific names

Many living things have a common name, but common names are not always exact. For instance, the common toad of Europe is different from a toad that is common in the Sonoran Desert of the United States and Mexico. Common names are also different in different languages.

To sort out such difficulties, scientists give every species a two-part Latin name. The first name is that of the genus the organism belongs to. The second is the name of the species within that genus. For example, the European common toad has the name *Bufo bufo* and the Sonoran Desert toad is *Bufo alvarius*. This way, scientists will not confuse the two species.

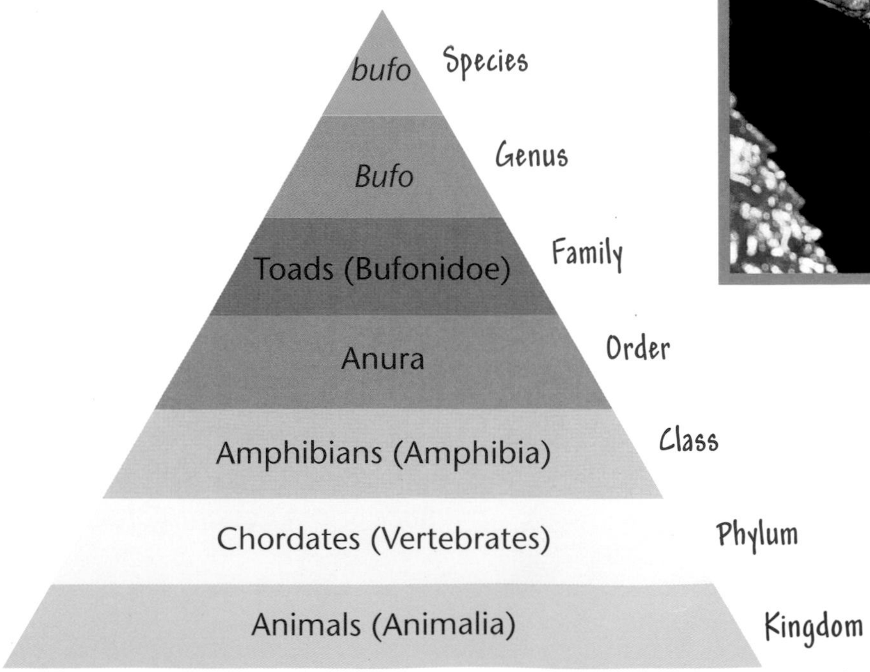

bufo Species

Bufo Genus

Toads (Bufonidoe) Family

Anura Order

Amphibians (Amphibia) Class

Chordates (Vertebrates) Phylum

Animals (Animalia) Kingdom

This diagram shows the classification for Bufo bufo—*a common toad.*

What Is an Amphibian?

There are three **orders** in the amphibian **class**: frogs and toads; newts and salamanders; and caecilians, which look like large worms with teeth. No matter how different these amphibian groups look, they all have several characteristics in common:

- Amphibians are **vertebrates.**
- Amphibians are cold-blooded, which means their bodies are only as warm as their surroundings.
- Amphibians have naked skin. Unlike other vertebrates, their skin has no covering of **scales,** hair, or feathers.
- Amphibians **reproduce** using eggs. Young amphibians usually look completely different from adults. They undergo big changes as they develop. This process is called **metamorphosis.**

A final important characteristic is revealed in the name *amphibian,* which comes from Greek words meaning "double life." Amphibians usually spend the early part of their lives in water and the later part on land.

The importance of a backbone

A backbone is a tough, flexible rod inside vertebrates. Muscles pull against the backbone to move limbs and other bones. Bones, such as ribs and the skull, are connected to the backbone and protect internal organs, such as the heart and brain, from damage.

This great crested newt is a member of the Caudata order.

This table shows the orders of amphibians and gives some examples of the main **families** and **species**.

Name of order	Families	No. of species	Example
Anura (frogs and toads) Appearance: large head, four legs, no tail, longer hind legs than front legs	Tailed frogs (Ascaphidae)	2	*Ascaphus truei*
	Fire-bellied toads (Bombinatoridae)	10	*Bombina bombina*
	True toads (Bufonidae)	449	common toad
	Glass frogs (Centrolenidae)	136	emerald glass frog
	Poison-dart frog (Dendrobatidae)	201	strawberry poison-dart
	Tree frogs (Hylidae and Hyperoliidae)	812	White's tree frog
	Southern frogs (Leptodactylidae)	1088	leopard frog
	Mantellas (Mantellidae)	127	golden mantella
	Narrowmouth toads (Microhylidae)	330	Eastern narrowmouth
	Spadefoot toads (Pelobatidae)	11	plains spadefoot
	Tongueless frogs (Pipidae)	30	*Pipa pipa*
	True frogs (Ranidae)	716	goliath frog
	Mouth-brooding frogs (Rhinodermatidae)	2	*Rhinoderma darwinii*
	Burrowing toads (Rhynophrydinae)	1	Mexican burrowing toad
Caudata (salamanders and newts) Appearance: long body and tail, four or two equal-sized legs	Mole salamanders (Ambystomatidae)	30	tiger salamander
	Giant salamanders (Cryptobranchidae)	3	hellbender
	Lungless salamanders (Plethodontidae)	352	green salamander
	Mudpuppies and olms (Proteidae)	6	mudpuppy
	Newts and fire salamanders (Salamandridae)	62	great crested newt
	Sirens (Sirenidae)	4	lesser siren
Gymnophiona (Caecilians) Appearance: wormlike body, no legs	Cocle caecilians (Caeciliaidae)	109	rubber eel

The Amphibian Life Cycle

Almost all animals change size between birth and adulthood, but some do more than that—they completely change their shape as well. This transformation is called **metamorphosis.** For example, caterpillars are young insects that change into adult butterflies. Amphibians and fish are the only **vertebrates** to change by metamorphosis.

Life in water

Metamorphosis is easiest to see in frogs and toads, where the **larvae**—called tadpoles—have a completely different shape than the adults do. Adult frogs and toads usually lay their jelly-coated eggs in water or a moist place. When the young tadpoles hatch out of the eggs, they look like fish. They have long tails, which they use for swimming, and **gills** on their sides, which allow them to breathe **oxygen** in the water.

Tadpoles change in many ways as they grow up into frogs. Developing legs are an easy change to spot.

A frog's hind feet have **webbed** toes that it can use for swimming. This tadpole has developed all its legs and is almost ready to leave the water.

A tadpole's mouth is small and has rows of tiny teeth that it uses to grate bits of water plants to eat. As the tadpole eats more, it grows bigger and starts to change. First it develops hind legs, and then front legs start to appear. Its tail starts to shrink in size, and its head, mouth, and eyes grow bigger. It begins to look more like an adult toad or frog. It starts to hunt tiny animals in the water, and its stomach and intestines change shape, allowing it to digest this new food. The gills transform into **lungs** inside its body.

Life on land

When they eventually crawl out of the water, young frogs and toads are **adapted** in ways that help them live on land. Their strong legs allow them to hop and walk around. Their tails have mostly disappeared, because they no longer need to swim. They can breathe oxygen in the air using their lungs. Their vision is better in air than in water, which means they can hunt efficiently. Many frogs and toads have a long sticky tongue that they can flick out to grab quick-moving food.

Live birth

Metamorphosis also happens in salamanders and caecilians, but it is often less obvious than in frogs. Most caecilians and some salamanders and frogs retain their eggs inside their bodies. The eggs develop safely inside their mothers' bodies. When the larvae emerge from their mothers, they are miniature versions of their parents.

Amphibian Skin

In wet places, amphibians such as this toad absorb a lot of water through their skin. They get rid of some of the excess water by urinating a lot.

Skin without hair, **scales,** or feathers is one characteristic that sets amphibians apart from other **vertebrates.** Thin, bare amphibian skin has both advantages and disadvantages.

Getting enough water

Without the right amount of water, all animals will die. To get the right amount, they need to drink. But they also need to control how much water they lose through **urination** and **evaporation** from the skin. For example, reptiles can live in dry places by urinating very little and by having scales on their skin, which limits evaporation.

Amphibian skin has no covering to prevent water loss by evaporation. To help prevent water loss from their bodies, amphibians live in moist places and their skin produces **mucus** to help keep it moist. Surprisingly, most amphibians do not drink. They don't need to. Their thin skin can absorb water very easily from the water, soil, or air around them.

Under the skin

Under its outer protective layer, the inner layer of amphibian skin contains nerves, blood vessels, and **glands.** Glands are places where special fluids are made and released. Some amphibian glands make mucus, but others also make poisons—some deadly, some that just taste bad—to defend against **predators.**

Breathing

Amphibians are unusual among vertebrates, because they can use their skin for "breathing." **Oxygen** in the air or water around them enters blood vessels beneath the surface of their moist skin. Blood then carries the oxygen to parts of the body that need it. Some salamanders breathe using only their skin, but most amphibians use a combination of skin and either **lungs** or **gills** for breathing, depending on where they live.

Shiny mucus covers the skin of this spotted salamander. The mucus helps keep its skin moist for breathing.

Colors

Amphibians are different colors because they have blobs of **pigment** in their skin. Color is vital to many amphibians and other animals for safety. Some are **camouflaged**—predators cannot easily see them because they are a similar color or pattern to their backgrounds. Others are brightly colored as a warning that they are poisonous. This tells predators that their **prey** will taste bad. Some amphibians can even change color by changing the shape of their pigment blobs. White's treefrogs change color from green to brown as they move from leaf surfaces to darker backgrounds.

Shedding

After **metamorphosis**, amphibians regularly change their outer skin. This is called shedding. They do this because the skin becomes damaged or dry. A new layer of skin grows underneath the old one. Toads pull off their old skin like you'd take off a tight pullover shirt. The skin does not go to waste, however. Many types of amphibians eat their old skin.

Frogs

Frogs are one group of amphibians that do not have tails as adults. They are classified in the same **order** as toads because toads also have no tails as adults. More than 90 percent of the world's amphibian **species** are frogs and toads. They have so many characteristics in common—such as skeleton shape—that some tailless amphibians are called either toads or frogs.

What is a frog like?

Frogs usually have long, strong hind legs that they use for jumping, and **webbed** toes that help them swim. Their skin is smooth. They use the bulging, often large eyes on top of their wide heads to see all around. Frogs are the noisiest amphibians. Their sounds are made even louder by areas of skin in their throats, called vocal sacs, that bulge out and act like loudspeakers.

Widespread frogs

Two of the largest **families** of frogs are the true frogs (Ranidae), which contains more than 700 species, and the southern frogs (Leptodactylidae), which contains more than 1,000 species. Southern frogs live in Central and South America, the West Indies, and the southern United States. True frogs live in Africa, the United States, Canada, Europe, and Asia.

ear

A frog's sensitive ears are hidden under circle-shaped patches of skin, which act like our eardrums.

True frogs

True frogs are called "true" because they show all the typical frog characteristics—long hind legs, smooth skin, and webbed toes. They live in a wide range of **habitats,** from wet to dry and hot to cold. The goliath frog—the biggest frog in the world—lives in West Africa and can grow to 12 inches (30 centimeters) long and weigh more than 6 pounds (3 kilograms). The bullfrog is an aggressive **predator** that hunts and eats **prey** such as small mammals, fish, and ducklings.

Southern frogs

Southern frogs also come in many different sizes and display typical frog characteristics. The small barking frog gets its name from the call that males make to attract females to **breed,** which sounds like a dog barking. Bell's horned frogs are sometimes as big as large dinner plates. They have hornlike knobs over their skin and striking **camouflage** markings that help them catch their prey.

The horned frog will eat anything that fits into its enormous mouth. Here it is eating a mouse. Like other frogs and toads, it has no teeth to bite or chew, so it can press its eyes down to help swallow large prey.

Frosty frog

Some wood frogs live north of the Arctic circle. They survive the freezing winters by **hibernating** underground in a burrow. Although their body fluids freeze, their **cells** do not, because the large amount of sugar in their blood acts like antifreeze.

Tree frogs

Several frog **families** spend most of their lives in trees. They are classified as tree frogs because they have special **adaptations** that help them to live among the branches.

The red-eyed tree frog has vertical pupils similar to a cat's. The pupils open wide at night as the frog hunts for food.

Clinging on

Most tree frogs (families Hylidae and Hyperoliidae) are less than four inches (ten centimeters) long, with long, flat bodies and necks. All tree frogs have big feet with long toes, which help them balance and climb among leaves and branches. There is usually a large, flat disk at the end of each toe. These disks are sticky and help them cling on tightly as they climb. Tree frogs also have **cartilage** between the last two bones of each toe. This flexible tissue allows the toes to swivel as the frog moves its body, while keeping the toe disks stuck flat against the tree.

Night vision

Many tree frogs are nocturnal, which means they are active at night and rest during the day. They usually have large eyes that make use of any available light. This allows them to get around, find food, and avoid **predators** in the dark.

Variety show

Tree frogs live in a variety of places. Most of them live in warm, moist, tropical places, such as a rain forest, but some live in cooler, drier **habitats** such as Europe. Most tree frog species hunt insects, spiders, centipedes, and other small animals, but a few are vegetarians. One Brazilian species only eats fruit!

Many male tree frogs call out at night to attract females. Some have common names that describe their calls, such as peeper, chorus frog, or bird-voiced frog.

In hiding

Tree frogs are usually the color of the plants they live among. This **camouflages** them so predators cannot spot them. For example, North American tree frogs are bright green because they live among bright green plants. They also have patches of yellow on their skin, which look like patches of sunlight. This makes them even less visible among the leaves.

*Groups of gray tree frogs lay their eggs in foam nests on branches above streams. The nests, which the frogs make from their own **mucus**, hide and keep the eggs moist. When the eggs hatch, the **larvae** drop into the water below.*

Odd ones out

Some tree frogs never go near trees but are classified as tree frogs because they share certain characteristics of tree frogs, such as their skeletons. For example, the water-holding frog that lives in southern Australian deserts spends much of its life hidden underground to avoid the heat. It sheds its protective cocoon of skin when the soil gets wet after a rainstorm.

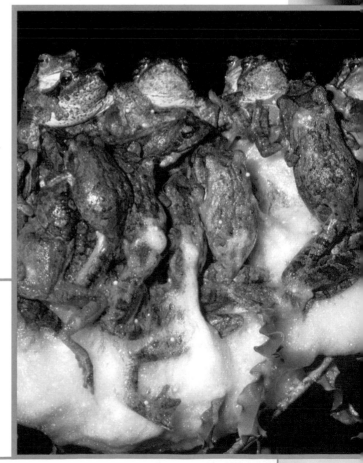

The poison in this tiny yellow poison-dart frog is so strong it could kill several humans.

Several other groups of frogs live in or near trees just as tree frogs do. They have different ways to help them avoid the attention of **predators.**

Bright sparks

The poison-dart frogs (**family** Dendrobatidae) of Central and South America and the mantellas (Mantellidae) of Madagascar are very small frogs, less than two inches (five centimeters) long. They live in tropical rain forests. The most striking thing about them is their appearance. Some are vivid yellow. Others are red with dark stripes, metallic green, or even bright blue. Their colors are an **adaptation.** They warn predators that their skin may be poisonous.

Frogs as weapons

Some South American people hunt animals high in trees using blowpipes and darts. They rub the dart tips with poison from a poison-dart frog. When the dart hits an animal, the poison kills it, and the animal drops down to the hunter below.

Poison-dart frogs make poison in special **glands** in their skin. The poison in some frogs is stronger in some frogs than in others. If a predator—such as a bird, snake, or spider—starts to eat a frog with weak poison, it will get a nasty taste in its mouth. If it eats a frog with strong poision it may die. Survivors remember to avoid these colorful frogs in the future.

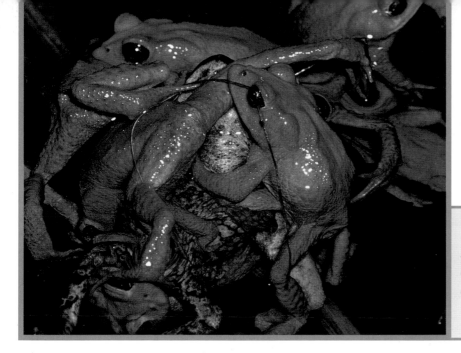

Male mantellas sometimes wrestle with each other over control of places to breed.

Colorful lives

Mantellas and poison-darts use their colors for other purposes too. In a shady rain forest, a brightly colored male is easier for a female to spot. Male mantellas patrol a territory that has small pools of water caught inside plants such as bamboo. After a female is attracted to a colorful male, she checks out his pools before choosing the right one in which to lay her eggs.

Females of some poison-dart **species** lay their eggs in nests made out of leaves on the forest floor. When the eggs hatch, the females carry their tadpoles to water, where they **metamorphose** into frogs. Some lay special eggs that have not been **fertilized** in the water for the tadpoles to feed on.

Flying frogs

Frogs of the family Rhacophoridae also live in trees. Wallace's flying frog can glide up to 50 feet (15 meters) from one tree to the next to escape danger. When it jumps, it spreads its large **webbed** feet out wide, which stretches the flaps of skin attached to its sides. The stretched skin forms a sort of parachute that keeps the frog from falling too fast. This allows it to get further away.

Special Frog Parents

There are four other different groups of frogs that have special ways of caring for their eggs and young tadpoles.

A tailed frog?

A general characteristic of adult frogs is that they do not have tails, but males of one **family** of frogs do appear to have them! In fact, the tail is a special tube used in **mating.** Tailed frogs (family Ascaphidae) use this unique tube to **fertilize** the female's eggs inside her body. The tube is an **adaptation** to life in rushing streams. In fast-moving water, eggs might be washed away before they can be fertilized.

Glass frogs

Glass frogs (family Centrolenidae) get their name from the transparent, or see-through, skin on their bellies. This is a type of **camouflage.** The color of the leaves or rocks they rest on shows through their skin, so they cannot be easily seen by **predators.** Some male glass frogs also use this camouflage to hide as they guard their eggs before they hatch. They have spotted skin on their backs so they resemble their eggs. If other frogs or small animals approach to eat their eggs, the glass frogs try to chase them off.

You can see the leaf this glass frog is resting on through its skin.

Surinam frog tadpoles hatch out of protected eggs on their mother's back.

Throat nursery

Mouth-brooding frogs (family Rhinodermatidae) are a group of small frogs that live in shady forest streams of South America. One of these, the female Darwin's frog, lays 20 to 30 eggs, which the male fertilizes and guards for two weeks. When the eggs are ready to hatch, he appears to eat them! In fact, the tadpoles go into his vocal sacs in his throat rather than in his stomach. They remain here, in safe hiding, until they have changed into small frogs. At this point, he opens his mouth and they hop away.

Keeping in contact

Tongueless frogs (family Pipidae) are **aquatic.** They always live in water. They use their tongueless mouths to suck up food from their muddy riverbed homes. One type, the Surinam frog, is incredibly flat and looks like a dead leaf. After her sticky eggs are fertilized, the female swims in loops in the water to catch them on her back. Over the next few days, the skin on her back swells around the eggs. This protects them as they develop into tadpoles.

This natterjack toad is a typical stubby toad shape. Its poison glands are near its eyes.

Toads are classified in the same **order** as frogs. Both have a similar shape, with longer hind legs than front legs and no tail, but there are some general differences.

How is a toad different from a frog?

Toads generally have shorter, stubbier bodies than frogs, with thick, dry, warty skin. Behind each eye is a swelling with tiny dimples that contains the toad's poison **glands.** All toads make poison—most of it not very strong—but only certain frogs make poison, such as poison-darts. Most toads have fairly drab-colored skin on their backs that **camouflages** them against the ground.

A toad's hind legs are usually shorter than those of frogs of similar size, and there is little **webbing** between its toes. Toads crawl slowly and hop, whereas frogs swim and leap. And toads generally lay their eggs in sticky strings rather than in clumps, as frogs do.

True toads

The common European toad is a true toad (**family** Bufonidae) because it clearly shows toad characteristics. It spends its days resting in shady, sheltered spots. At night it stalks **prey** such as slugs and worms, which it catches by flicking out its sticky tongue. If it eats something it does not like, it can vomit out its entire stomach and wipe it clean before tucking it back!

Earth movers

Several families of toads have features that help them dig. Spadefoot toads (family Pelobatidae) have tough, spade-shaped feet with hardened pads. They use these to dig backward into soil, forming burrows. Burrows underground are cool and moist and keep spadefoot toads out of the sight of **predators**.

Narrowmouth toads (family Microhylidae) got their name from the fact that their large bellies make their heads look narrow. The Eastern narrowmouth toad of the United States lives in sandy soil that is easy to dig into. It feeds mostly on ants at night, when it is cooler. It can roll forward a fold of skin on its neck to protect its eyes from ant bites and stings.

Advance warning

Many toads defend themselves from predators by using poison in their skin. Some toads have extra tricks. The fire-bellied toad (family Bombinatoridae) has a green or brown camouflaged back, but its stomach is bright red or orange. The camouflage hides it from most predators. But if danger gets too close, it flashes its stomach. This is a warning to predators to keep away because it is poisonous.

When the Mexican burrowing toad (family Rhinophrynidae) is alarmed, it blows up like a balloon to look bigger than it really is.

spade-shaped back foot

Salamanders

At first sight, most salamanders look like lizards. They have small heads with rows of small teeth, bright skin, long tails, and short legs set at right angles to their bodies. However, salamanders are amphibians. Unlike lizards, which are reptiles, salamanders have no **scales** on their skin and no claws on their toes, and they need moist places in which to **breed**. Around 500 **species** of salamanders have been identified and classified into ten different groups.

The female great crested newt hides each egg in the leaf of a water plant until it hatches.

Newts are salamanders

Newts are some of the most familiar salamanders. They are rough-skinned, long-legged members of just one **family** of salamanders—Salamandridae. Other members of this family include the yellow and black fire salamanders.

Male newts put on displays to attract females for breeding. The male great crested newt, for example, develops a jagged crest along his back and a silver color on his tail. Then he swims while wiggling his tail in front of the female. This encourages her to lay her eggs, which he then **fertilizes**.

Telling tails

If a **predator** catches a salamander by the tail, the salamander can let its tail fall off. This gives it a chance to get away. A new tail can grow back. Salamanders can also regrow some other damaged or severed body parts.

Different changes

When fire salamander **larvae** hatch out of their eggs, they look similar to their parents. As they grow, they do not change much except in size.

Newt larvae look much less like their parents when they hatch than salamanders do. At first they have **gills** and no legs, similar to tadpoles. As they grow, the front legs and then the hind legs develop, and the gills change into **lungs.** Following **metamorphosis,** the young newt leaves the water to live on land until it is old enough to **reproduce.**

Heavy build

Mole salamanders (family Ambystomatidae) all have thick bodies, blunt heads, small eyes, and flat tails. Their name comes from their good digging ability. At up to 16 inches (40 centimeters) long, the tiger salamander is the largest salamander on land. It comes out at night and uses its good sense of smell to hunt worms, mice, insects, and other amphibians.

Tiger salamander larvae are less than half of an inch long when they hatch. They eat so much that they grow ten times bigger over the next twelve weeks.

Second change

Just after metamorphosis, Eastern newts are called efts. An eft's bright red skin serves as a warning to predators about the poison it contains. After several years growing up on land, the eft changes color to brown and develops a flat tail that it uses for swimming. Although still poisonous, the eft is then an adult, ready to return to the water to breed.

Other salamanders can be divided into two main groups: **aquatic** and lungless. Aquatic salamanders always live in or next to water. Lungless salamanders live in a variety of damp **habitats**.

Eternal youth

Adults of many aquatic salamander **families** look the same as their **larvae**. They have the same features that help them to breathe and swim as their larvae do, because they also live in water. Grown-up mudpuppies and olms (family Proteidae), for example, have feathery **gills** on their sides and **fins** at the tops and bottoms of their tails. The olm lives in pools in dark caves. It is blind and has pinkish-white skin and a long snout, which it uses to smell **prey** such as worms.

Adult hellbenders and giant salamanders (family Cryptobranchidae) have gills inside their bodies, hidden behind slits. These amphibians have wide heads and wrinkled fleshy skin. They live in fast-flowing, rocky rivers and shelter in long burrows under riverbanks.

Sirens (family Sirenidae) have long eel-like bodies and just two (front) legs. Unlike other aquatic salamanders, they have both gills and **lungs** after **metamorphosis**.

Mudpuppies never transform entirely. They reach 8 to 18 inches (20 to 45 centimeters) long but never lose their red gills.

Without lungs

There are around 350 **species** of lungless salamanders (family Plethodontidae). Most live in North and Central America. They do not have lungs or gills. Instead, they breathe through their skin and the lining of their mouths. Most lungless salamanders are quite small—less than 6 inches (15 centimeters) long. A few species live permanently in water, but most live in damp places on land, near streams, among moss, or under stones.

Lungless salamanders eat small prey such as insects, slugs, and woodlice. Adults usually feed at night and spend the day hiding. Most lungless salamanders can see quite well, but they usually find their prey by sensing vibrations from the ground. They also use their sharp senses of smell and taste, which they feel through their sensitive tongue. The Shasta salamander can shoot out its long sticky tongue almost the full length of its body to catch prey such as flies.

High and low

Lungless salamanders can live in very different places. Some live in caves or wells very deep underground. Others live in trees, many feet above the ground.

*The arboreal salamander (a lungless salamander) climbs trees using broad, flat, **webbed** feet and a prehensile, or gripping, tail. It makes its home in old birds' nests.*

Caecilians

Caecilians (pronounced suh-SILL-yuns) are amphibians that never have legs. They look like worms or snakes, but they are classified as amphibians because they have characteristics such as smooth, slimy skin with no **scales.** A caecilian's skin forms tough raised rings along its long, thin body.

There are more than 150 **species** of caecilians, divided into five groups. Most are black or pale, although some are brightly colored. Caecilians range in size from a few inches to more than three feet (one meter) long, and they live in warm places, such as Mexico, Southeast Asia, and parts of Africa.

Going underground
Most types of caecilians live in underground burrows. They usually burrow headfirst into soft earth, forcing a path with their hard skulls. The rings on their bodies, like those on an earthworm, help them get a grip as they move through the soil.

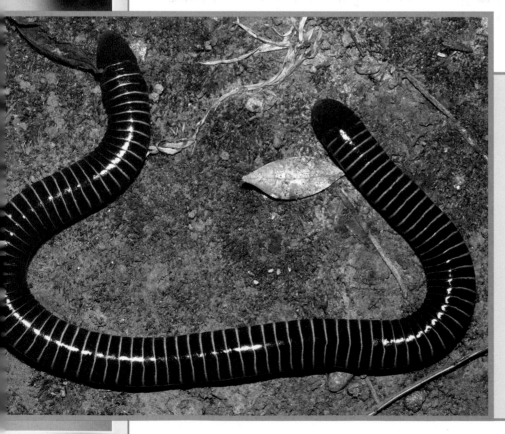

This blue caecilian looks like a large earthworm. Unlike worms, caecilians have a skeleton inside their bodies and teeth inside their jaws. They also have a tentacle beneath their eyes, which helps them detect prey in their dark burrows.

Caecilians' small eyes are usually covered with skin, and often by bone too, so they are nearly blind.

The lives of caecilians

Scientists have been unable to study caecilians in detail, because the animals live most of their lives underground. Caecilians come to the surface only when they have to—for example, to keep from drowning if rain floods their burrows.

Caecilians are carnivores, or meat-eaters, eating small underground **prey** such as earthworms and termites. Their main **predators** are large, burrowing snakes. Caecilians are thought to live alone most of the time, coming together only to **mate**.

A male caecilian, unlike other male amphibians, **fertilizes** the female's eggs inside her body. **Larvae** of many species hatch from the eggs inside their mothers and are then born live. Other caecilians lay eggs in nests and carefully guard their eggs and young.

Caecilian divers

Fishermen in the muddy waters of South American rivers often catch the **aquatic** caecilians, commonly called rubber eels. They have flat bodies and a small tail **fin**, so they are often mistaken for fish called eels. Their skin is wrinkly and provides a large enough surface for skin-breathing in the muddy water.

Pioneers of Water and Land

The first **vertebrates** to live on land were amphibians. Scientists believe that more than 350 million years ago—long before the dinosaurs—a few fish started to use their **fins** to crawl out of the sea. On the wet mud of the shore they could catch many insects to eat and then go back into the water. Over time their **descendants adapted** in ways that allowed them to live on land. Eventually they became so different from fish that we consider them to be a different type of animal—amphibians. These amphibians, like those of today, returned to the water when it was time to breed. Their eggs and **larvae,** like those of fish, could develop properly only if moist.

One of a Kind

Amphibians are a unique **class** of vertebrates. Although the class contains a wide range of different shapes and sizes, they all have a distinct combination of the characteristics that make them amphibians. Other groups of animals may have one of these characteristics, but no other group has all of them together.

*Eels are very similar in shape to caecilians. However, unlike amphibians, eels have **gills**, scales on their skin, and many other characteristics of fish.*

Tricky classification

Classifying amphibians is not always straightforward. For example, mole salamanders look like lizards called skinks. But, on closer inspection, skinks—unlike salamanders—have dry, **scale**-covered skin. But classifying animals based on just one characteristic can be difficult. For example, some lizard **species** have very smooth skin with scales so tiny they are difficult to see, so they could be mistaken for amphibians. Individual animals also vary, just like humans. Some amphibians are differently sized, differently colored, or differently shaped from others in the same species.

Examining a range of characteristics is necessary for classification because some amphibians do things differently. As we have seen through this book, some frogs lay their eggs on land instead of in water, and some salamanders never **metamorphose.** But all amphibians have more characteristics in common with each other than with any other type of animal.

Same solution

Different types of animals often look the same because they have the same features that help them to live in the same **habitat.** For example, caecilians look like big worms. Both animals have smooth, slippery skin and segment rings. And, both are blind because both spend their lives burrowing through the soil.

Glossary

adaptation special feature that helps an organism to survive in its habitat

aquatic living in water

breed to produce babies

camouflage color, shape, or pattern that disguises an animal against its background

cartilage rubbery tissue that is softer than bone

class level of classification grouping between phylum and order. Amphibians make up a class.

descendant later generation of a type of organism

evaporation process by which liquid water changes to vapor

family level of classification grouping between order and genus

fertilize when male sex cells join with female sex cells so they can develop into larvae

fin flap of skin with or without bones in it that helps an animal swim

genus (plural is **genera**) level of classification grouping between family and species

gill structure used for breathing underwater

gland part of an animal's body that produces and releases particular fluids

habitat place where an organism lives

hibernate to sleep through the winter

larva (plural is **larvae**) stage of amphibian life between birth and adulthood

lung body structure found in most vertebrates used for breathing in air

mate to come together to produce babies

metamorphose to undergo the process of metamorphosis

metamorphosis process of change from larva shape to adult shape

mucus slime

order level of classification grouping between class and family. There are three orders of amphibians.

organism living thing

oxygen gas that most organisms breathe

phylum (plural is **phyla**) level of classification grouping between kingdom and class

pigment substance that causes color

predator animal that hunts and eats other animals

prey animal that is hunted and eaten by another animal

reproduce to have babies

scale overlapping or interlocking piece that forms a protective layer over reptile and fish skin

species lowest level of classification grouping. Only members of the same species can reproduce together.

urination process of ridding the body of liquid waste

vertebrate animal with an internal backbone. All amphibians are vertebrates.

webbed describes skin that is stretched between two toes to help with swimming

More Books to Read

Parker, Steve. *Adaptation.* Chicago: Heinemann Library, 2000.

Stewart, Melissa. *Amphibians.* Danbury, Conn.: Children's Press, 2001.

Wallace, Holly. *Classification.* Chicago: Heinemann Library, 2000.